NICE
LITTLE TOWN
EASTER

D1825365

Adult coloring book

BY

TANYA BOGEMA (STOLOVA)

Our group in facebook:
https://www.facebook.com/groups/1280996941971412/

Hi! My name is Tatiana and I'm painter :)
Thank you so much that you are choosing my books in spite of many other books present on market. I really appreciate this. Every time I start new project I think about how to make my book more interesting. And I can't do this without you. To do that I need to have your feedbacks. Communication with you is very very important for creation process. With your feedbacks you give me new ideas and inspiration for new books that become better and more interesting.
Sincerely yours, Tatiana.

Nice Little Town Easter - Adult Coloring Book

Copyright © 2017 by Tatiana Bogema (Stolova)

ISBN: 978-1984190499

THIS BOOK BELONGS TO

Jeni Pruitt

2019 .

ILLUSTRATIONS
FROM
OTHER
MY
BOOKS

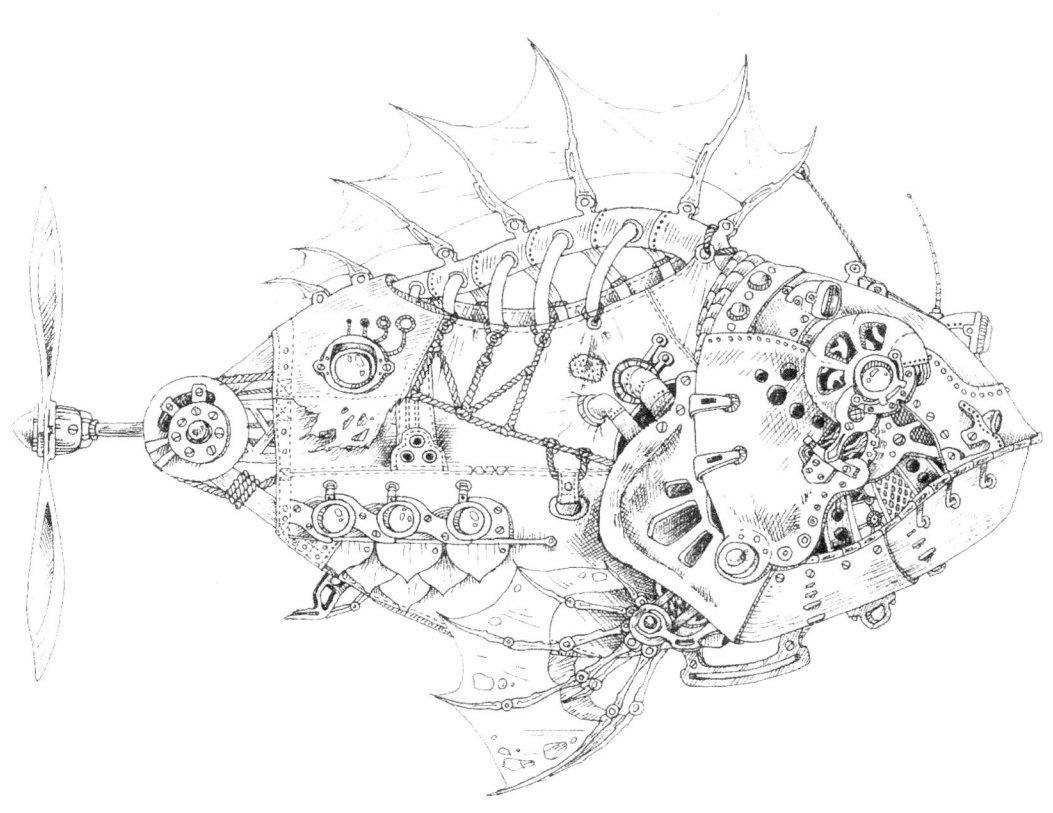

CUTE GIRLS

MAGIC
MASK

GREAT
LIONS

STEAMPUNK

STEAMPUNK

VOL 2

AWESOME
ANIMALS

NICE
LITTLE TOWN
CHRISTMAS

NICE LITTLE
DRAGONS

FOR VALENTINE, WITH LOVE!

Printed by Amazon Italia Logistica S.r.l.
Torrazza Piemonte (TO), Italy

10315982R00066